LIFE IS MESSY—
GOD IS GOOD
GRATITUDE JOURNAL

Every day, every moment, God reaches into your life with His hand of grace to help you through all that you face. It's His way of saying, "Be assured. I know you are weak, but I am strong. Rest in My power and let My grace take over where your efforts end."

There isn't anything He can't do or accomplish through you, so be glad and rejoice in knowing that no matter how messy your life gets, He is more than able to pick up the pieces.

Life is messy

GOD IS GOOD

GRATITUDE JOURNAL

DaySpring

LIVE YOUR FAITH

> Joys that prompt a thankful heart
> flow from the goodness of God.
> **—BONNIE JENSEN**

I AM *thankful* FOR...   DATE

May the God of hope fill you
with all joy and peace.

ROMANS 15:13 CSB

Thankfulness is the quickest path to joy.

—JEFFERSON BETHKE

I AM *thankful* FOR...   DATE

Give thanks to the LORD, for He is good!
His faithful love endures forever.

PSALM 107:1 NLT

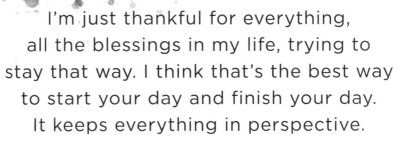

I'm just thankful for everything,
all the blessings in my life, trying to
stay that way. I think that's the best way
to start your day and finish your day.
It keeps everything in perspective.

—TIM TEBOW

I AM *thankful* FOR...   DATE

And give thanks
for everything to God.

EPHESIANS 5:20 NLT

Faith does not concern itself
with the entire journey.
One step is enough.
—LETTIE COWMAN

I AM *thankful* FOR...   DATE

●

●

●

I will bless you...
and you will be a blessing.

GENESIS 12:2 CSB

This is true faith, a living confidence
in the goodness of God.
—MARTIN LUTHER

I AM *thankful* FOR...   DATE

Throw yourselves into the work of the Master,
confident that nothing you do for Him
is a waste of time or effort.

I CORINTHIANS 15:58 THE MESSAGE

Often God has to shut a door in our face so that He can subsequently open the door through which He wants us to go.

—CATHERINE MARSHALL

I AM *thankful* FOR...   DATE

Those who have reason to be thankful
should continually sing praises to the Lord.

JAMES 5:13 TLB

Look for the goodness of God all around you. As you look for signs of His Presence, many more opportunities will occur for you to bless people and share God's true nature.

—GRAHAM COOKE

I AM *thankful* FOR...   DATE

The LORD gives His people strength;
the LORD blesses His people with peace.

PSALM 29:11 CSB

When you're feeling grateful, look up—
because God has again smiled on you
through someone special who cared.
—MATT ANDERSON

I AM *thankful* FOR...   DATE

May the LORD smile on you
and be gracious to you.

NUMBERS 6:25 NLT

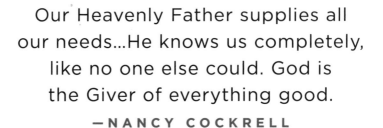

> Our Heavenly Father supplies all our needs...He knows us completely, like no one else could. God is the Giver of everything good.
>
> **—NANCY COCKRELL**

I AM *thankful* FOR...   DATE

God will supply all your needs according
to His riches in glory in Christ Jesus.

PHILIPPIANS 4:19 CSB

It is not how much we have, but how much we enjoy, that makes happiness.

—CHARLES SPURGEON

I AM *thankful* FOR...   DATE

God...provides us with all things to enjoy.

I TIMOTHY 6:17 CSB

A moment of gratitude makes a
difference in your attitude.
—BRUCE WILKINSON

I AM *thankful* FOR...   DATE

Give thanks to the LORD, for He is good;
His faithful love endures forever.

PSALM 118:29 CSB

No matter what our circumstances,
we can find a reason to be thankful.
—DR. DAVID JEREMIAH

I AM *thankful* FOR...   DATE

Love never gives up, never loses faith, is always hopeful, and endures through every circumstance.

I CORINTHIANS 13:7 NLT

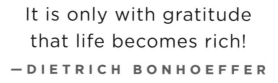

It is only with gratitude
that life becomes rich!
—DIETRICH BONHOEFFER

I AM *thankful* FOR... DATE

Pray diligently...with your eyes wide open in gratitude.

COLOSSIANS 4:2 THE MESSAGE

Anticipate the future and its changes with joy. There is a seed of God's love in every event, every circumstance.

—BARBARA JOHNSON

I AM *thankful* FOR...   DATE

● _____

   _____

   _____

   _____

● _____

   _____

   _____

   _____

● _____

   _____

   _____

   _____

God be with you!...And God bless you!

RUTH 2:4 THE MESSAGE

Gratitude brings joy and laughter
into your life and into the lives
of all those around you.
—EILEEN CADDY

I AM *thankful* FOR... DATE

I am trusting You, O LORD, saying,
"You are my God!"
My future is in Your hands.

PSALM 31:14, 15 NLT

Every volcano is a powerful illustration
of God's character. He is a Vesuvius
of goodness, life, and energy.
—REINHARD BONNKE

I AM *thankful* FOR...   DATE

LORD, there is no one like You! For You are great, and Your name is full of power.

JEREMIAH 10:6 NLT

The very fact that a holy, eternal,
all-knowing, all-powerful, merciful,
fair, and just God loves you and me
is nothing short of astonishing.

—FRANCIS CHAN

I AM *thankful* FOR...   DATE

God can pour on the blessings in astonishing ways.

II CORINTHIANS 9:8 THE MESSAGE

The Christian does not think
God will love us because we are
good, but that God will make us
good because He loves us.

—C.S. LEWIS

I AM *thankful* FOR...   DATE

Nothing in all creation will ever be able
to separate us from the love of God.

ROMANS 8:39 NLT

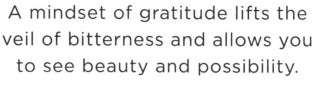

> A mindset of gratitude lifts the
> veil of bitterness and allows you
> to see beauty and possibility.
> **—STEVE MARABOLI**

I AM *thankful* FOR...   DATE

Don't worry about anything, but in everything,
through prayer and petition with
thanksgiving, present your requests to God. And the
peace of God, which surpasses all understanding,
will guard your hearts and minds in Christ Jesus.

PHILIPPIANS 4:6-7 CSB

Yesterday is forgotten, today
is in His hands, and tomorrow
is filled with His promises.
—SUSAN GESELL

I AM *thankful* FOR...   DATE

The LORD always keeps His promises;
He is gracious in all He does.

PSALM 145:13 NLT

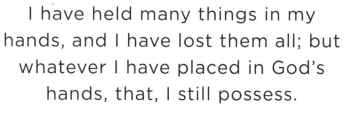

I have held many things in my hands, and I have lost them all; but whatever I have placed in God's hands, that, I still possess.

—CORRIE TEN BOOM

I AM *thankful* FOR...   DATE

I trust You, LORD,
and I claim You as my God.
My life is in Your hands.

PSALM 31:14-15 CEV

Love, joy, peace, patience, kindness,
goodness, faithfulness, gentleness,
and self-control. To these I commit my day.
If I succeed, I will give thanks. If I fail, I will seek
His grace. And then, when this day is done,
I will place my head on my pillow and rest.

—MAX LUCADO

I AM *thankful* FOR...   DATE

He brings gifts into our lives, much the same way
that fruit appears in an orchard—things like affection
for others, exuberance about life, serenity.

GALATIANS 5:22 THE MESSAGE

It's one thing to be grateful. It's another to give thanks. Gratitude is what you feel. Thanksgiving is what you do.

—TIM KELLER

I AM *thankful* FOR...   DATE

Let your lives overflow
with thanksgiving
for all He has done.

COLOSSIANS 2:7 TLB

We can see hope in the midst of hopelessness. We can see peace in the midst of chaos.

—PRISCILLA SHIRER

I AM *thankful* FOR...   DATE

_____

_____
_____
_____
_____

_____

_____
_____
_____
_____

_____

_____
_____
_____
_____

We know that God causes everything to work together for the good of those who love God and are called according to His purpose for them.

ROMANS 8:28 NLT

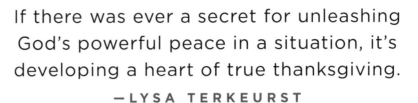

If there was ever a secret for unleashing God's powerful peace in a situation, it's developing a heart of true thanksgiving.

—LYSA TERKEURST

I AM *thankful* FOR...

DATE

Don't worry about anything, but in everything,
through prayer and petition with
thanksgiving, present your requests to God. And the
peace of God, which surpasses all understanding,
will guard your hearts and minds in Christ Jesus.

PHILIPPIANS 4:6-7 CSB

God is able to do what we can't do.

—BILLY GRAHAM

I AM *thankful* FOR...   DATE

Trust in the LORD with all your heart,
and do not rely on your own understanding;
in all your ways know Him,
and He will make your paths straight.

PROVERBS 3:5-6 CSB

In the happy moments—we'll thank Him.
In the busy moments—we'll bless Him.
In the trying moments—we'll trust Him.
In the quiet moments—we'll praise Him.

—ROY ANDERSON

I AM *thankful* FOR...   DATE

O Lord, You...know everything about me.
You know when I sit down or stand up.
You know my every thought when far away.
You chart the path ahead of me
and tell me where to stop and rest.
Every moment You know where I am.

PSALM 139:1-3 NLT

Gratitude paints little smiley
faces on everything it touches.
—RICHELLE E. GOODRICH

I AM *thankful* FOR...   DATE

Give thanks to the LORD and proclaim His greatness.
Let the whole world know what He has done.

PSALM 105:1 NLT

Thankfulness is the
antidote to bitterness.
—SUSAN GOSS

I AM *thankful* FOR...   DATE

Praise the LORD! Give thanks to the LORD,
for He is good! His faithful love endures forever.

PSALM 106:1 NLT

Thank You, Lord, for being patient
with me. For it's so hard to see,
when my eyes are on me.

—KEITH GREEN

I AM *thankful* FOR...   DATE

Rest in the LORD, and wait patiently for Him.

PSALM 37:7 KJV

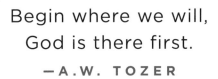

Begin where we will,
God is there first.

—A.W. TOZER

I AM *thankful* FOR...   DATE

And God is able to make every grace
overflow to you, so that in
every way, always having everything you
need, you may excel in every good work.

II CORINTHIANS 9:8 CSB

God knows. God sees.
God cares. He's there.
—TONY EVANS

I AM *thankful* FOR...   DATE

God cares...right down to the last detail.

JAMES 5:11 THE MESSAGE

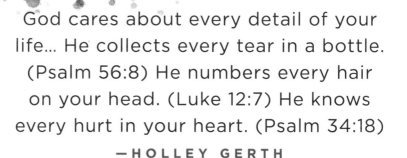

God cares about every detail of your life... He collects every tear in a bottle. (Psalm 56:8) He numbers every hair on your head. (Luke 12:7) He knows every hurt in your heart. (Psalm 34:18)

—HOLLEY GERTH

I AM *thankful* FOR...   DATE

If God cares so wonderfully for flowers
that are here today and gone tomorrow,
won't He more surely care for you?

MATTHEW 6:30 NLT

Since it doesn't cost a dime to dream,
you'll never shortchange yourself
when you stretch your imagination.
—ROBERT SCHULLER

I AM *thankful* FOR...   DATE

We are more than conquerors
through Him who loved us.

ROMANS 8:37 CSB

> To be grateful is to recognize the love of God in everything He has given us— and He has given us everything.
>
> **—THOMAS MERTON**

I AM *thankful* FOR...   DATE

God cares for you.

I PETER 5:7 CEV

Pray about BIG THINGS... Pray about SMALL THINGS... Because God cares about ALL THINGS in your life.

—ROY LESSIN

I AM *thankful* FOR...   DATE

I am able to do all things through
Him who strengthens me.

PHILIPPIANS 4:13 CSB

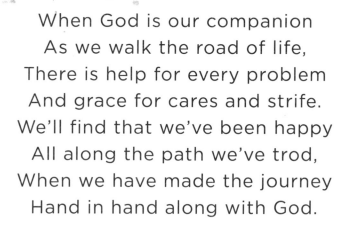

When God is our companion
As we walk the road of life,
There is help for every problem
And grace for cares and strife.
We'll find that we've been happy
All along the path we've trod,
When we have made the journey
Hand in hand along with God.

—JON GILBERT

I AM *thankful* FOR...   DATE

I trust You, LORD,
and I claim You as my God.
My life is in Your hands.

PSALM 31:14, 15 CEV

A grateful heart recognizes
that all of life is a gift.
—ADAM HAMILTON

I AM *thankful* FOR...   DATE

Teach us to number our days, that we
may apply our hearts unto wisdom.

PSALM 90:12 KJV

Joy is the direct result of having God's perspective on our daily lives and the effect of loving our Lord enough to obey His commands and trust His promises.

—BILL BRIGHT

I AM *thankful* FOR...

DATE

Every good and perfect gift is from above,
coming down from the Father of lights.

JAMES 1:17 CSB

Gratitude unlocks the fullness
of life. It turns what we have
into enough, and more.

—MELODY BEATTIE

I AM *thankful* FOR...   DATE

Take delight in the LORD,
and He will give you your heart's desires.

PSALM 37:4 CSB

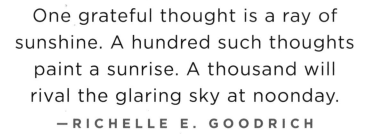

One grateful thought is a ray of
sunshine. A hundred such thoughts
paint a sunrise. A thousand will
rival the glaring sky at noonday.

—RICHELLE E. GOODRICH

I AM *thankful* FOR...   DATE

You reveal the path of life to me;
in Your presence is abundant joy.

PSALM 16:11 CSB

We are all on our way somewhere.
We'll get there if we just keep going.

—BARBARA JOHNSON

I AM *thankful* FOR...   DATE

Blessed be His glorious name forever;
the whole earth is filled with His glory.

PSALM 72:19 CSB

Joy comes from
knowing God loves me.
—DR. JAMES DOBSON

I AM *thankful* FOR...   DATE

Surely Your goodness and unfailing love
will pursue me all the days of my life.

PSALM 23:6 NLT

God, give us the grace to accept with serenity the things that cannot be changed, the courage to change the things that should be changed, and the wisdom to distinguish the one from the other.

—REINHOLD NIEBUHR

I AM *thankful* FOR...   DATE

I have learned how to be content with whatever I have.

PHILIPPIANS 4:11 NLT

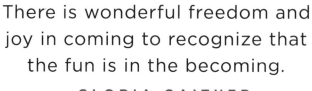

There is wonderful freedom and
joy in coming to recognize that
the fun is in the becoming.

—GLORIA GAITHER

I AM *thankful* FOR...   DATE

I will bless you with a future filled with hope.

JEREMIAH 29:11 CEV

God knows not only what we need but also when we need it. His timing is always perfect.
—ELISABETH ELLIOT

I AM *thankful* FOR...   DATE

I am the LORD your God,
who teaches you what is good for you
and leads you along the paths you should follow.

ISAIAH 48:17 NLT

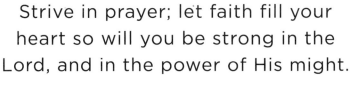

Strive in prayer; let faith fill your
heart so will you be strong in the
Lord, and in the power of His might.

—ANDREW MURRAY

I AM *thankful* FOR...   DATE

May Your faithful love rest on us, LORD,
for we put our hope in You.

PSALM 33:22 CSB

Gratitude is the ability to experience life as a gift. It liberates us from the prison of self-preoccupation.

—JOHN ORTBERG

I AM *thankful* FOR...   DATE

You reveal the path of life to me;
in Your presence is abundant joy.

PSALM 16:11 CSB

> We can thank God for the simple gifts of grace He gives us every day.
> —SHEILA WALSH

I AM *thankful* FOR...   DATE

God has given each of you a gift from
His great variety of spiritual gifts.
Use them well to serve one another.

1 PETER 4:10 NLT

Our favorite attitude
should be gratitude.
—**ZIG ZIGLAR**

I AM *thankful* FOR...   DATE

You are the God of miracles and wonders! You still demonstrate Your awesome power.

PSALM 77:14 TLB

Gratitude can transform common days into thanksgivings, turn routine jobs into joy, and change ordinary opportunities into blessings.

—WILLIAM ARTHUR WARD

I AM *thankful* FOR...   DATE

Oh, the joys of those who trust the LORD.

PSALM 40:4 NLT

Replace worry with prayer. Make the decision to pray whenever you catch yourself worrying.

—ELIZABETH GEORGE

I AM *thankful* FOR...   DATE

Don't worry about anything; instead,
pray about everything. Tell God what you need.

PHILIPPIANS 4:6 NLT

Happiness depends on what happens; joy does not.
—OSWALD CHAMBERS

I AM *thankful* FOR...   DATE

God is my helper;
the Lord is the sustainer of my life.

PSALM 54:4 CSB

Faith does not occupy itself with
outward things; it is an act of the will...
an inward choice that says,
"I believe, though I don't see.
I trust, though I can't understand."
—GWEN FAULKENBERRY

I AM *thankful* FOR...   DATE

Faith is the confidence that what we
hope for will actually happen; it gives us
assurance about things we cannot see.

HEBREWS 11:1 NLT

God is the silent partner in
all great enterprises.
—ABRAHAM LINCOLN

I AM *thankful* FOR...

DATE

Encourage one another!

ISAIAH 41:6 NLT

When we put our hope and trust in God, we find that His faithfulness is unmistakable, His goodness is unrelenting, and His prodigal love is constant no matter what.

—JAMI PIERCE

I AM *thankful* FOR...   DATE

May Your faithful love rest on us, LORD,
for we put our hope in You.

PSALM 33:22 CSB

God does not love us because
we are valuable. We are valuable
because God loves us.

—FULTON SHEEN

I AM *thankful* FOR...   DATE

Even the very hairs of your
head are all numbered.
Fear not therefore: ye are of more
value than many sparrows.

LUKE 12:7 KJV

When trouble comes, focus on
God's ability to care for you.
—CHARLES STANLEY

I AM *thankful* FOR...   DATE

God is our refuge and strength,
always ready to help in times of trouble.

PSALM 46:1 NLT

There is never a time when we may not hope in God. Whatever our necessities, however great our difficulties, and though to all appearance help is impossible, yet our business is to hope in God, and it will be found that it is not in vain.

—GEORGE MUELLER

I AM *thankful* FOR...   DATE

God can point to us in all future ages
as examples of the incredible wealth of
His grace and kindness toward us.

EPHESIANS 2:7 NLT

> God uses ordinary people
> who are obedient to Him to
> do extraordinary things.
> —JOHN MAXWELL

I AM *thankful* FOR...   DATE

No power in the sky above or in the earth below—
indeed, nothing in all creation will ever be
able to separate us from the love of God that
is revealed in Christ Jesus our Lord.

ROMANS 8:39 NLT

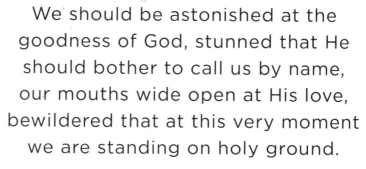

We should be astonished at the goodness of God, stunned that He should bother to call us by name, our mouths wide open at His love, bewildered that at this very moment we are standing on holy ground.

—BRENNAN MANNING

I AM *thankful* FOR...   DATE

By His divine power, God has given us everything we need for living a godly life. We have received all of this by coming to know Him, the one who called us to Himself by means of His marvelous glory and excellence.

II PETER 1:3 NLT

Every day we live is a priceless gift of
God, loaded with possibilities to learn
something new, to gain fresh insights.

—DALE EVANS ROGERS

I AM *thankful* FOR...   DATE

The LORD will always guide you.

ISAIAH 58:11 CEV

When you experience the challenges
of life, perspective is everything.
—JONI EARECKSON TADA

I AM *thankful* FOR...   DATE

The Lord will provide what is good.

PSALM 85:12 CSB

Kindness is no small thing.
—TRIESTE VAILLANCOURT

I AM *thankful* FOR...   DATE

Your kindness has often
refreshed the hearts
of God's people.

PHILEMON 1:7 NLT

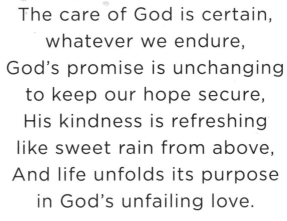

The care of God is certain,
whatever we endure,
God's promise is unchanging
to keep our hope secure,
His kindness is refreshing
like sweet rain from above,
And life unfolds its purpose
in God's unfailing love.

—BARBARA LOOTS

I AM *thankful* FOR...   DATE

It's in Christ that we find out who we are and what we are living for. Long before we first heard of Christ...He had His eye on us, had designs on us for glorious living, part of the overall purpose He is working out in everything and everyone.

EPHESIANS 1:11, 12 THE MESSAGE

Thankfulness is a key to your life. It is the key that turns your situation around because it changes you, your outlook, and your attitude. There is power in a thankful heart!

—ANN WOODRUFF

I AM *thankful* FOR...   DATE

Blessed be the God and Father of our Lord Jesus Christ, the Father of mercies and the God of all comfort.

II CORINTHIANS 1:3 CSB

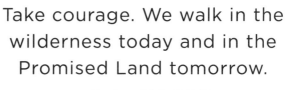

Take courage. We walk in the
wilderness today and in the
Promised Land tomorrow.
—D.L. MOODY

I AM *thankful* FOR...   DATE

Be brave. Be strong. Don't give up.

PSALM 31:24 THE MESSAGE

There's not much you can't achieve or endure if you know God is walking by your side.

—BILL HYBELS

I AM *thankful* FOR...   DATE

This is the day the Lord has made;
let us rejoice and be glad in it.

PSALM 118:24 CSB

The truth is, God's strength
is fully revealed when our
strength is depleted.

—LIZ CURTIS HIGGS

I AM *thankful* FOR...   DATE

God...will supply all your needs
from His glorious riches.

PHILIPPIANS 4:19 NLT

Fill up the spare moments of your
life with praise and thanksgiving.

—SARAH YOUNG

I AM *thankful* FOR...   DATE

Be still, and know that I am God!

PSALM 46:10 NLT

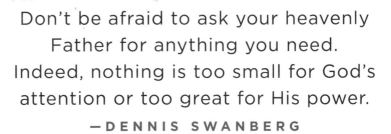

Don't be afraid to ask your heavenly
Father for anything you need.
Indeed, nothing is too small for God's
attention or too great for His power.

—DENNIS SWANBERG

I AM *thankful* FOR...   DATE

How we thank God for you! Because of you we
have great joy as we enter God's presence.

1 THESSALONIANS 3:9 NLT

"Little things"
have big potential
with God.
—RICH DAVIS

I AM *thankful* FOR...   DATE

Nothing is impossible with God.

LUKE 1:37 NLT

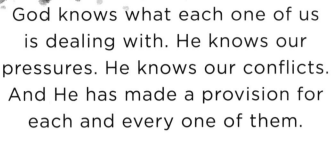

God knows what each one of us
is dealing with. He knows our
pressures. He knows our conflicts.
And He has made a provision for
each and every one of them.
—KAY ARTHUR

I AM *thankful* FOR...   DATE

May Your faithful love rest on us, LORD,
for we put our hope in You.

PSALM 33:22 CSB

> If we fill our lives with simple good
> things and constantly thank God
> for them, we will be joyful.
>
> **—RICHARD J. FOSTER**

I AM *thankful* FOR...   DATE

Think about all you can praise God
for and be glad about.

PHILIPPIANS 4:8 TLB

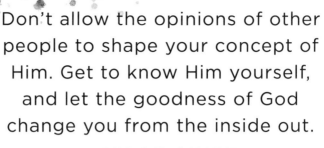

Don't allow the opinions of other people to shape your concept of Him. Get to know Him yourself, and let the goodness of God change you from the inside out.

—JUDAH SMITH

I AM *thankful* FOR...   DATE

His promise was true...
His purposes never change...
These things...give us strength
to hold on to the hope
we have been given.

HEBREWS 6:17, 18 NCV

Don't worry—I've got this.

—GOD

I AM *thankful* FOR...   DATE

With God's power working in us, God can do much,
much more than anything we can ask or imagine.

EPHESIANS 3:20 NCV

Do all the good you can. In all the
ways you can. In all the places
you can. At all the times you can.
To all the people you can.
—JOHN WESLEY

I AM *thankful* FOR... DATE

If your faith
is as big as a mustard seed,
you can say to this mountain,
"Move from here to there,"
and it will move. All things
will be possible for you.

MATTHEW 17:20 NCV

The more you give, the more comes back to you, because God is the greatest giver in the universe, and He won't let you out give Him. Go ahead and try. See what happens.

—RANDY ALCORN

I AM *thankful* FOR...   DATE

Give, and you will receive. Your gift will return to you in full—pressed down, shaken together to make room for more, running over, and poured into your lap. The amount you give will determine the amount you get back.

LUKE 6:38 NLT

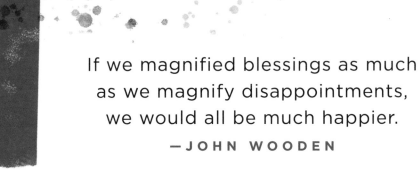

If we magnified blessings as much
as we magnify disappointments,
we would all be much happier.

—JOHN WOODEN

I AM *thankful* FOR...   DATE

Let Your people be happy
and celebrate because of You.

PSALM 68:3 CEV

When we determine to dwell on the good and excellent things in life, we will be so full of those things that they will tend to swallow our problems.

—RICHARD J. FOSTER

I AM *thankful* FOR...   DATE

The LORD has blessed me because of you.

GENESIS 30:27 NLT

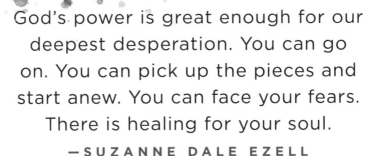

God's power is great enough for our deepest desperation. You can go on. You can pick up the pieces and start anew. You can face your fears. There is healing for your soul.

—SUZANNE DALE EZELL

I AM *thankful* FOR...   DATE

Surely Your goodness and unfailing love
will pursue me all the days of my life.

PSALM 23:6 NLT

Don't worry about tomorrow.
God is already there.

—(IN)COURAGE

I AM *thankful* FOR...   DATE

I am convinced that nothing can ever
separate us from God's love.

ROMANS 8:38 NLT

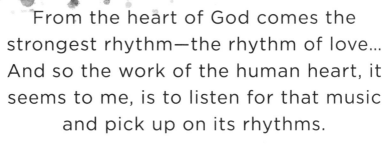

From the heart of God comes the strongest rhythm—the rhythm of love... And so the work of the human heart, it seems to me, is to listen for that music and pick up on its rhythms.

—KEN GIRE

I AM *thankful* FOR...   DATE

May grace and peace be multiplied to you through the knowledge of God and of Jesus our Lord.

II PETER 1:2 CSB

Just hang on—God's got a grand
view in His plan for you!

—JULIE SAWYER

I AM *thankful* FOR...   DATE

You, LORD God, have done many wonderful things, and You have planned marvelous things for us. No one is like You! I would never be able to tell all You have done.

PSALM 40:5 CEV

Every morning is a
chance at a new day.
—MARJORIE HINCKLEY

I AM *thankful* FOR... DATE

Let's celebrate and be glad today.

PSALM 118:24 CEV

Gratitude therefore takes nothing for granted, is never unresponsive, is constantly awakening to new wonder and to praise of the goodness of God.

—THOMAS MERTON

I AM *thankful* FOR...   DATE

Teach us to make the most of our time,
so that we may grow in wisdom.

PSALM 90:12 NLT

The earth under your feet, the rain over your face upturned, the stars spinning all around you in the brazen glory: this is for you, you, you. These are for you...so count the ways He loves, a thousand, more, never stop.

—ANN VOSKAMP

I AM *thankful* FOR...   DATE

This is how God showed His love to us:
He sent His one and only Son
into the world so that
we could have life through Him.

1 JOHN 4:9 NCV

This is one of those days when we can look back, taste, see, and know that God is good and love is winning.

—SARAH MUELLER

I AM *thankful* FOR...   DATE

No doubt about it! God is good.

PSALM 73:1 THE MESSAGE

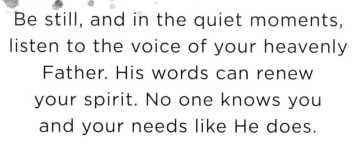

Be still, and in the quiet moments, listen to the voice of your heavenly Father. His words can renew your spirit. No one knows you and your needs like He does.

—JANET L. SMITH

I AM *thankful* FOR...   DATE

How grateful I am, and how I praise the Lord.

PHILIPPIANS 4:10 TLB

When you walk... God will steady you.
When you run... He will sustain you.
And when you fly...yes, when you fly—
He will take you places you never dreamed.

—LINN CARLSON

I AM *thankful* FOR...   DATE

But those who trust in the Lord will find new strength.
They will soar high on wings like eagles.
They will run and not grow weary.
They will walk and not faint.

ISAIAH 40:31 NLT

For God is, indeed, a wonderful Father who longs to pour out His mercy upon us, and whose majesty is so great that He can transform us from deep within.

I AM *thankful* FOR...   DATE

Create in me a clean heart, O God;
and renew a steadfast spirit within me.

PSALM 51:10 NKJV

You who have received so much love share it with others. Love others the way that God has loved you, with tenderness.

—MOTHER TERESA

I AM *thankful* FOR...   DATE

Dear friends, since God loved us as much as that, we surely ought to love each other too. For though we have never yet seen God, when we love each other God lives in us, and His love within us grows ever stronger.

I JOHN 4:11-12 TLB

God is not only the answer to
a thousand needs, He is also
the answer to a thousand wants.
He is the fulfillment of our chief
desire in all of life. For whether
or not we've ever recognized it,
what we desire is unfailing love.

—BETH MOORE

I AM *thankful* FOR...   DATE

God promises to love me all day, sing songs
all through the night! My life is God's prayer.

PSALM 42:8 THE MESSAGE

> You are God's created beauty and the focus of His affection and delight.
>
> —JANET WEAVER SMITH

I AM *thankful* FOR...   DATE

Be beautiful inside, in your hearts,
with the lasting charm of a gentle and
quiet spirit that is so precious to God.

I PETER 3:4 TLB

Life is Messy—God is Good Gratitude Journal
© 2019 DaySpring Cards, Inc. All rights reserved.
First Edition, August 2019

Published by:

P.O. Box 1010
Siloam Springs, AR 72761
dayspring.com

Unless otherwise noted, all Scripture quotations are taken from
the Christian Standard Bible®, Copyright © 2017 by Holman Bible
Publishers. Used by permission. Christian Standard Bible® and CSB
are federally registered trademarks of Holman Bible Publishers.

Scripture quotations marked NLT are taken from the Holy Bible,
New Living Translation, copyright © 1996, 2004, 2007, 2013, 2015
by Tyndale House Foundation. Used by permission of Tyndale House
Publishers, Inc., Carol Stream, Illinois 60188. All rights reserved.

Scripture quotations marked THE MESSAGE are taken from
The Message. Copyright © 1993, 1994, 1995, 1996, 2000, 2001,
2002. Used by permission of NavPress Publishing Group.

Scripture quotations marked NCV are taken from the New Century Version®.
Copyright © 2005 by Thomas Nelson, Inc. Used by permission. All rights reserved.

Scripture quotations marked CEV are taken from the Contemporary English
Version. © 1991, 1992, 1995 by American Bible Society. Used by permission.

Scripture quotations marked KJV are taken from the Holy Bible, King James Version.

Scripture quotations marked TLB are taken from The Living Bible
copyright © 1971. Used by permission of Tyndale House Publishers,
Inc., Carol Stream, Illinois 60188. All rights reserved.

Cover design by Lauren Purtle
Printed in China
Prime: 93058
ISBN: 978-1-644-54309-2